Cheatum

Cheatum

THE PHILIPPINES

A TRUE BOOK®

by

Shirley Wimbish Gray

Children's Press®
A Division of Scholastic Inc.

New York Toronto London Auckland Sydney
Mexico City New Delhi Hong Kong
Danbury, Connecticut

A Philippine boy

Content Consultant
Matthew Holman
*Center for Southeast
Asian Studies
University of Wisconsin-
Madison
Madison, WI*

Reading Consultant
Nanci R. Vargus, Ed.D.
*Assistant Professor
Literacy Education
University of Indianapolis
Indianapolis, IN*

Dedication
To Wayne, Jeffrey and Travis

*The photograph on the
cover shows rice terraces in
Luzon. The photograph on
the title page shows
children displaying the shells
they found.*

Library of Congress Cataloging-in-Publication Data

Gray, Shirley Wimbish.
    The Philippines : / by Shrirley Wimbish Gray.
        p. cm. — (A true book)
    Summary: Explores the geography, history, people, and culture of the
Philippines.
    Includes bibliographical references and index.
    ISBN 0-516-24212-1 (lib. bdg.)   0-516-27775-8 (pbk.)
    1. Philippines—Juvenile literature. [1. Philippines.] I. Title. II. Series.
DS655 .G73 2003
959.9—dc21   2002005898

CHILDREN'S PRESS, AND A TRUE BOOK®, and associated logos are
trademarks and or registered trademarks of Grolier Publishing Co., Inc.
SCHOLASTIC and associated logos are trademarks and or registered
trademarks of Scholastic Inc.

1 2 3 4 5 6 7 8 9 10 R 12 11 10 09 08 07 06 05 04 03

Contents

A Country of Many Islands   5

The People of the Philippines   16

Spanish Missionaries
    and Colonial Rule   21

Struggles for Independence   27

Life in the Philippines Today   34

To Find Out More   44

Important Words   46

Index   47

Meet the Author   48

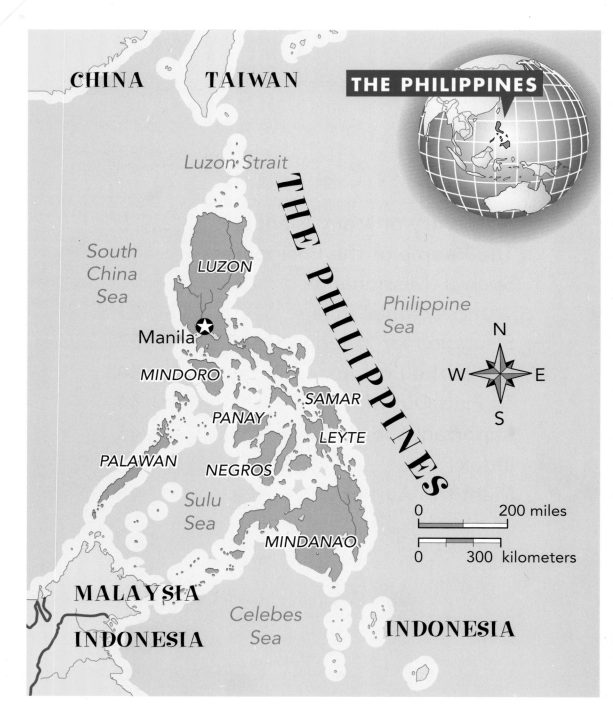

CHINA TAIWAN

THE PHILIPPINES

Luzon Strait

South
China
Sea

LUZON

THE PHILIPPINES

Philippine
Sea

Manila

MINDORO

SAMAR

PANAY

LEYTE

PALAWAN

NEGROS

Sulu
Sea

N

W   E

S

0   200 miles

0   300 kilometers

MINDANAO

MALAYSIA

Celebes
Sea

INDONESIA

INDONESIA

A Country of Many Islands

The Philippines is a country made up of a chain of more than 7,100 islands. The chain sits in the western Pacific Ocean. Some of the islands are so small that no one can live on them. Other islands have large mountain ranges, valleys, and rivers.

Borneo is the nearest neighbor to the Philippines. It is only about 25 miles (40 km) from the southern tip of the islands. The Philippine islands are located southeast of Hong Kong and northeast of Indonesia. The South China Sea lies to the north and west of the Philippines. The Celebes Sea is to the south and the Philippines Sea is on the east.

A group of islands like the Philippines is called an **archipelago**. If all the islands

This island is part of the Philippine archipelago.

were put together, the Philippines would be about the size of Arizona. These thousands of islands are the tops of mountain ranges that lay on the bottom of the ocean. Volcanoes formed the mountains.

The Philippines has two main seasons, each with extreme weather conditions. Monsoon winds bring rain during the summer, from May until November. The winter months of December through April are dry.

Flooding is common in the Philippines during the wet season.

The temperature is warm all year, averaging about 80°F (27°C). Sometimes heavy storms called typhoons hit the islands. A *typhoon* is like a hurricane with strong winds. It causes much flooding.

The largest of the Philippine islands is Luzon. On its eastern coast is the city of Manila. It is the capital and largest city in the Philippines. Most of the other major cities are also located on the islands' coasts.

Manila is one of the busiest cities in the Philippines.

Ships transport goods to and from the coastal cities.

These seaports are centers of trade. Boats sailing in and out of these ports carry products made in the Philippines to other countries.

Thick **mangrove** swamps grow along the coasts. The swamps are home to reptiles and amphibians such as pythons, monitor lizards, and tree frogs. The trees on the islands also provide shelter to parrots and hornbills. Many scientists visit the smaller islands to study endangered species of birds. Beautiful **orchids** grow wild on the islands. Most tourists describe the Philippines as a tropical paradise.

Volcanoes

Sometimes the ground moves in the Philippines. Why? Earthquakes and volcanic eruptions shake the islands. One of the most active volcanoes is Mount Mayon. It is shaped like a cone and glows at night.

A volcanic crater in the Philippines

Mount Pinatubo is another active volcano. It is on the island of Luzon. For more than six hundred years, Mount Pinatubo was asleep, or inactive. Suddenly it began erupting in 1991. It sent huge clouds of ash and steam into the air for several days. Today, scientists know that twenty volcanoes on the islands remain active. That means that they are likely to erupt soon.

The eruption of Mount Pinatubo in 1991

The People of the Philippines

The first people to live on the Philippine islands may have come from China. They probably traveled over a land bridge that no longer exists. Large groups of Malayan people also came to the Philippines. Most of the Malayan people became

Many children can speak both Philipino and English.

Christians. Today these native people are called Filipinos.

Philipino is also the name of the official language of the Philippines. Some people also spell it Filipino. It is based on an old language called Tagalog.

Most Filipino children speak English in the classroom. Businesses and the government also use English.

Most Filipinos are Roman Catholic. The remaining people are either Protestant Christian or Muslim. Each January thousands of Roman Catholics gather in Manila. They come for the Festival of the Black Nazarene. Huge crowds of men take turns carrying a life-size statue of Jesus through the streets.

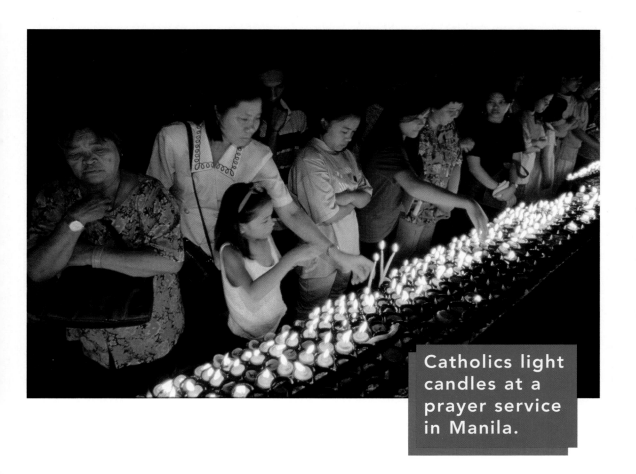

Catholics light candles at a prayer service in Manila.

The statue is made of **blackwood**. Church bells ring and fireworks explode during the procession.

Corazon Aquino was the first female president of the Philippines.

The people of the Philippines elect their president. This person serves as the leader of the government. In 1986, the Philippines elected Corazon Aquino as the first woman to serve as president.

Spanish Missionaries and Colonial Rule

Ferdinand Magellan was a Spanish explorer. He tried to find a new route to the east for Spain. During his travels, he landed on one of the Philippine islands. He built a cross near the modern seaport

Ferdinand Magellan of Spain (above) was an early visitor to the islands. Tourists can visit Magellan's cross in Cebu (right).

of Cebu. Later a local chief named Lapu-Lapu led a group of warriors who killed Magellan in a battle. Tourists can visit the remains of Magellan's cross today.

The Philippines was named after King Philip II of Spain.

Spain continued to send explorers across the ocean. In 1542, Spanish explorers claimed the islands for Spain. They named them the Philippine Islands in honor of King Philip II.

Roman Catholic **missionaries** soon followed the explorers. They taught the native people about Christianity.

The Philippines remained under Spanish control through most of the 1800s. Spain also ruled other countries such as Cuba and Puerto Rico. Life was hard under Spanish rule. The Philippine people wanted to be independent. Some of their leaders began to fight the Spanish.

Troops march through the Philippines before the Spanish-American War.

In 1898, the United States fought Spain in the Spanish-American War. Later that year,

the Spanish fleet was anchored in Manila Bay. The Philippines helped the United States attack it. Spain soon gave the Philippines to the United States in exchange for $20 million.

Struggles for Independence

The United States controlled the Philippine islands for about 45 years. During this time, the Philippines elected some of the leaders for their government. But the leader of the country was appointed by the United States. The Philippine people still wanted to rule themselves.

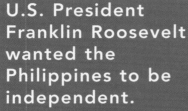
U.S. President Franklin Roosevelt wanted the Philippines to be independent.

When Franklin Roosevelt was elected president of the United States in 1932, he agreed with the Philippine people. The country needed to be independent. Soon the Philippine people wrote a **constitution**. They also elected their own president. Then World War II began. Japanese planes attacked the Philippines before the islands could become independent. Japan took over the country.

Japanese tanks invaded the Philippines during World War II.

In 1945, the United States helped free the Philippines from the Japanese. One year later, on July 4, 1946, the American flag was lowered and replaced by The Republic of the Philippines flag. The new country was established and the Philippines was finally independent!

The new country agreed to let the United States keep military bases on the islands for many years. Many American soldiers served there at Clark

Air Force Base and at Subic Bay Naval Base. The United States closed its last base on the islands in 1992.

In 1965, the Philippine people elected Ferdinand Marcos president. Many problems developed

Philippine president Ferdinand Marcos

while he was president. Marcos decided not to follow the constitution. He became a very wealthy and powerful leader. But the Philippine people did not want Marcos leading their country. They wanted to elect a new president. Finally, in 1986, Marcos was forced to leave the country. He died in Hawaii a few years later.

The Philippine government still struggles today. Several Muslim groups have staged

Filipinos vote during an election.

revolts in recent years. But the
Philippine people still hold elections.
They still decide who is in charge
of their own government.

Life in the Philippines Today

Life in the Philippines today includes traditions from many different countries. For example, restaurants serve Spanish and Chinese foods. At home, families eat rice at most meals. Roasted fish or meat is usually the

Rice and fish are common ingredients in Philippine dishes.

main course. Dessert often includes rice cooked with sweet milk.

Many children play baseball and basketball just like children in the United States. Sipa is also popular. It is like volley-ball, but players do not use their hands. Instead they can only use their feet and legs.

Family life is important to the Philippine people. Almost one half of the people live on small family farms. Rice is the most important crop.

Many Filipinos are farmers.

Stairway to the Sky

Rice terraces

Rice usually grows in flat fields that can be flooded easily. So how can farmers living in the Philippine mountains grow it? On the island of Luzon, farmers grow rice on **terraces**. These flat fields were carved into the steep hillsides thousands of years ago. Nearby streams help flood the terraces.

Filipinos planting rice

Farmers also grow sugarcane and tobacco to sell to other countries. Fruits such as pineapples, oranges, mangoes, and bananas are also important exports.

Farming is not the only way to earn money. Many craftsmen make baskets and furniture from bamboo and rattan. These are also sold to other countries. This has become an important industry for the Philippines.

Thousands of tourists visit the Philippines each year. Its coastline is larger than that of the United States and beach activities are

41

popular. Scuba diving is a favorite pastime. Divers enjoy exploring the coral that lives off the shores of the islands.

While traveling in the Philippines, many tourists ride in jeepneys. What is a jeepney? It is a cross between a jeep and a bus! After World War II, the Filipinos painted the army jeeps that were left on the island. Then they used them for transportation. When they ran out of those jeeps, they

Colorful jeepneys are
a fun way to travel
around the cities.

started making new ones.
Colorful jeepneys are a popular
way of getting around the
streets of Manila.

To Find Out More

Here are some additional resources to help you learn more about the Philippines:

Books

Aguilar-Cariño, Maria Luisa B. **Cordillera Tales.** Quezon City: New Day, 1990

Brittan, Dolly. **The People of the Philippines.** New York: PowerKids Press, 1998.

Krasno, Rena and Illeana Lee. **Kneeling Carabao and Dancing Giants: Celebrating Filipino Festivals.** Berkeley, CA: Pacific View Press, 1997.

Paterno, Maria Elena and Albert Gamos. **The Girl Who Fell from the Sky and Other Classic Philippine Legends.** Manila: Tahanan Books for Young Readers, 1993.

Organizations and Online Sites

Pinatubo Volcano
ph.net/htdocs/pinatubo

http://park.org/Phillipines/ pinatubo/index.html

Information about Pinatubo and other volcanoes in the Philippines.

Riceworld
www.riceworld.org

Find out how rice is grown in the Philippines and around the world.

Philippine Mission to the United Nations
Philippine Mission Center, 5th Floor
556 Fifth Ave.
New York, NY   10036
http://www.undp.org/ missions/philippine/

Find fast facts about natural resources, geography, and the people of the Philippines.

Important Words

archipelago a group of islands

blackwood a hardwood tree with a dark color

constitution the laws of a nation that describe the rights of the people and the power of the government

mangroves small trees and bushes that grow in shallow salt water

missionary someone sent to do religious work in another country

orchid a tropical flower

terrace a series of flat ridges built into a hillside

Index

(**Boldface** page numbers
   indicate illustrations.)

animals, 13
Aquino, Corazon, 20, **20**
archipelago, 6, **7**
bamboo, 40
basketball, 36, **36**
baskets, 40, **41**
birds, 13
Cebu, 22
christianity, 24
colonial rule, 21–26
coral, 42
daily life, 34–43
election, 29, 31, 33, **33**
farming, 37, **37,** 40
Festival of the Black
   Nazarene, 18–19
Filipinos, 17
flooding, **9,** 10, 39
food, 34–35, 40
furniture, 40, **41**
government, 27, 30–33
independence, 27–33
Japan, 29–30
jeepney, 42–43, **43**
King Philip II, 23, **23**
language, 17–18
Luzon, 10, 15, 39

Magellan, Ferdinand,
   21–22, **22**
mangrove swamps, 13
Manila, 10, **11,** 18, **19,** 26,
   26, 43
Marcos, Ferdinand, 31–32,
   31
military bases, 30–31
missionaries, 21–26
monsoons, 8
Mount Mayon, 14
Mount Pinatubo, 15, **15**
orchids, 13
people, 16–20
president, 20, **20,** 29
rattan, 40
rice, 34–35, 37, 38–39, **38, 39**
Roman Catholics, 18, **19,** 24
Roosevelt, Franklin, 28, **28**
scuba diving, 42
seasons, 8
sipa, 36
Spain, 21–26
Spanish-American War, 25–26
sports, 36
tourists, 13, 41–42
Typhoons, 10
United States, 25, 26, 27–30
volcanoes, 8, 14–15, **14, 15**
World War II, 29

Meet the Author

Shirley Wimbish Gray, MA, has been a writer and educator for more than 20 years. In addition to writing children's books, she coordinates cancer education at the University of Arkansas for Medical Sciences. She also consults with scientists and doctors about their writing. She lives in Little Rock, Arkansas, with her husband and two sons.